House of Cards:
The Heart Suit

by Denise Weaver Ross

The original versions of *Rafting the River, Cerulean Blue* and *Heart Transplant* were originally published in the *Sunday Poem: Ditchrider Blog* on dukecityfix.com on June 9, 2013.

*For my sons, Alex and Nick,
in memory of their father, Colin,
and my father, Ken, and the others
who appear here as seen by my inner eye.*

The poems in this book are not explanations of the artwork — nor does the art necessarily illustrate the poems — sometimes there is a direct connection and other times there is a resonance between the two. I have provided brief notes where it seemed appropriate.

I like to think of it being similar to point and counterpoint in music...

~ Denise Weaver Ross

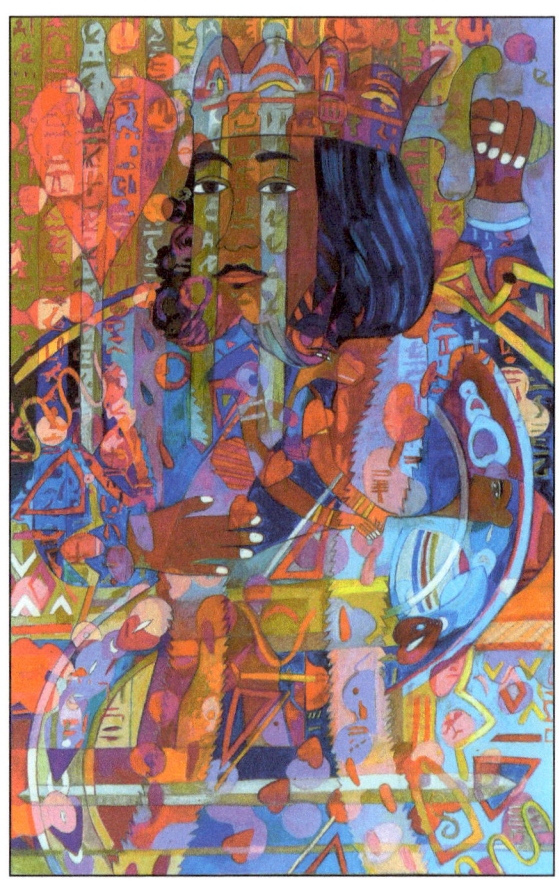

The King of Pain and the Sickle Moon
40 x 26 inches, 2012

This card was inspired by my late husband who died in 2001 from complications of sickle cell disease,
a lifelong blood disorder that causes bouts of severe pain. The card has a background pattern created
by sickled blood and also refers to Egyptian mythology. The poem ends with his and my father's deaths
(one year apart), and the first three stanzas refer to the near-death experiences of our two sons.

Cerulean Blue

Pain is the blue of hospital gowns,
stripes on a newborn baby blanket.

Pain codes blue with alarms, thunders
with pairs of white sneakers down long
corridors, shivers under navy hospital
covers, waiting to hold a baby swollen –
alien with countless wires and tubes.

Pain turns lips from purple to indigo
in a driveway waiting for sirens to grow
louder than the thundering of my heart.

Pain pulsates in blue fluorescent lights
in the silence of an emergency room
when the monitors have gone still.

Pain is the cerulean blue of summer skies,
high and hot above ashes in a rose garden.

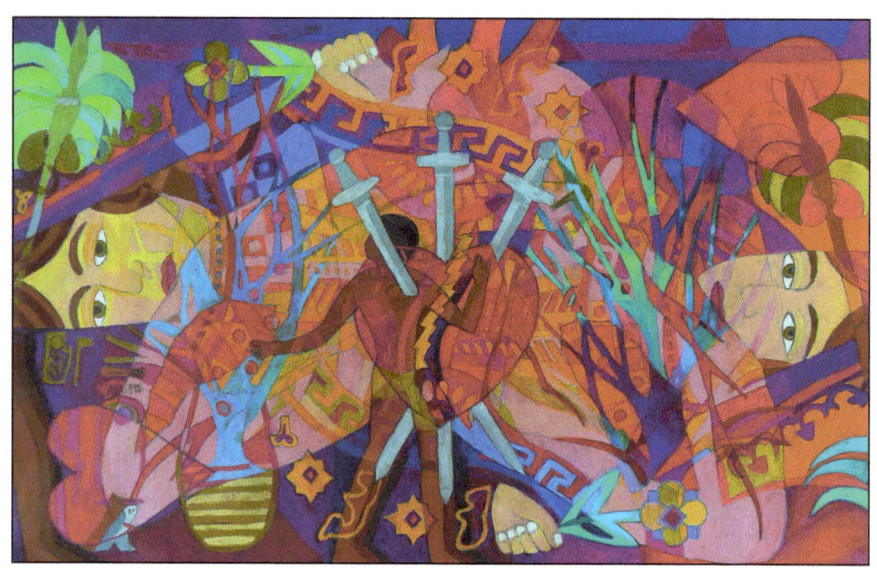

The Queen of Heart Transplants
26 x 40 inches, 2012

The poem was a response to a friend going through a painful divorce and the card explores
my metaphorical heart transplant after the death of my husband. Parts of the poem are "found"
and quoted directly from the University of California's "Patient's Guide to Heart Transplant Surgery."

Heart Transplant

You must prepare yourself
for the operation. This may take
a long time, and there is no guarantee
that a donor heart will be found.

Abstinence, therapy, and meditation
are recommended; avoid drugs and
an excess of alcohol, which will only
make your heart's problems worse.

If you find a compatible donor heart,
cut in between your ribs, forcing
your ribcage open, leaving your
damaged heart exposed but beating.

Connect your circulatory system
to the heart-lung machine; breathe.

Stop your heart.

Slice open the protective pericardium
and remove your heart, leaving only
the back part of your left atrium.

Trim and reshape the donor heart;
fit the new heart into what remains.

With luck, your donor heart
will start beating. Disconnect
the machine; remember to breathe.
Give yourself time to recover;
take your anti-rejection medication.

You have survived, taken a risk,
been given a gift. Choose joy.

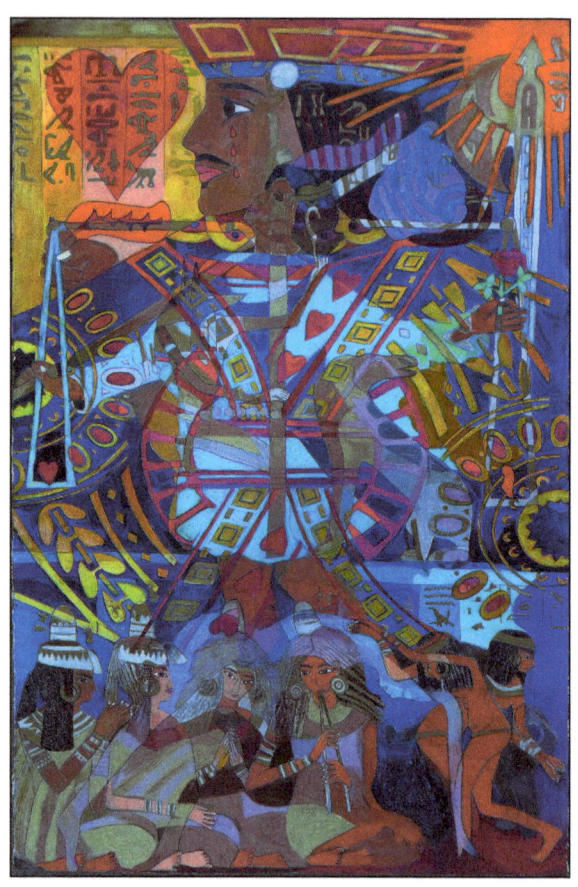

Jack of Lonely Hearts
40 x 26 inches, 2012

*The card plays with the connotations of the "Jack of Hearts" and the "Fool" from the Tarot –
a young man playing with love and getting burned in the process. The poem refers to my husband,
who was a popular DJ and dancer in Jamaica in his youth. The "Doctor Bird" is a distinctive
hummingbird found only in Jamaica. It has been said the name is due to its black crest and long tails
that resemble the top hat and frock coat worn by the English doctors during colonial times.*

Walk Like An Egyptian

When we met, it was one of many tunes
we laughed about, sang and danced to –
and you could dance like an Egyptian
or a belly dancer, your slim hips undulating,
eyes sparkling; all you needed was a veil.

In Jamaica you drove the girls mad and
they would chant your name. When we visited
they flocked around you, cooing like pea doves,
but you were the Doctor Bird – all you needed
was a top hat, coat and tails.

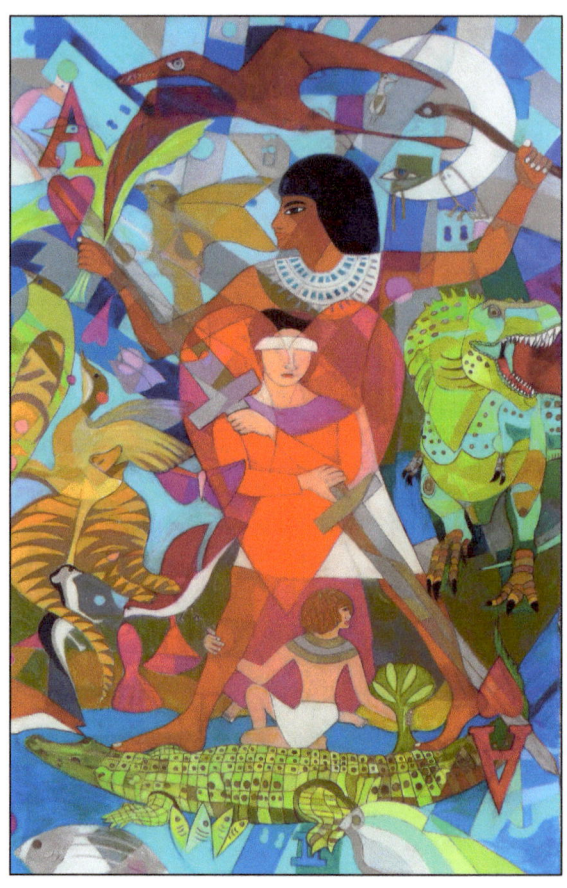

Ace of My Heart
40 x 26 inches, 2012

The card and poem are about my eldest son who suffers from Type I diabetes. In the card, I am the blindfolded figure in the middle trying to protect him from all the unseen dangers, and his brother, the supporting figure helping him maintain his balance on a crocodile. In the card diabetes test-strips form the background and he is surrounded by the prehistoric creatures he was fascinated with throughout his childhood – the poem reflects my understanding of his fascination with the Godzilla series.

Godzilla

Great protector of the nuclear age
inhabits my son's dreams
along with Mothra, Rodan and King Ghidorah.

Glorious monsters
summoned to protect a nation, a world,
a boy from those unspeakable dangers:

Radiation, racism and war.

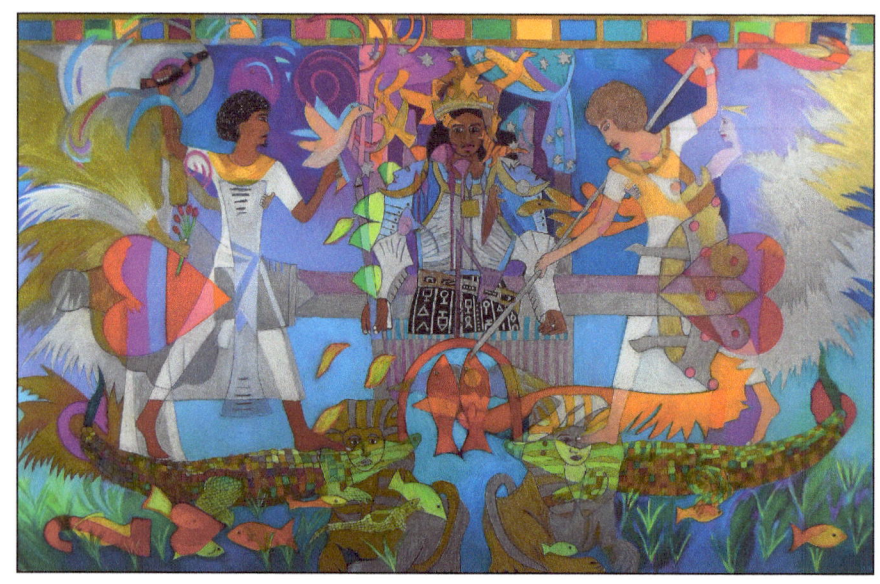

Two of Brotherly Love
26 x 40 inches, 2012

The two brothers are my two sons with their father providing the charioteer in the middle.
The brothers are supported by their guardian angels on their precarious crocodile rides through life.
The figures are inspired by Egyptian tomb paintings which I use throughout this series because
of their preoccupation with mortality and their stunning depictions of people of color.
The poem was written about my youngest son's response to the terrible Indonesian Tsunami.

Tsunami

The years are ending and beginning
with earthquakes and tsunamis:
12,000, 56,000, 144,000 and more are dead.
Lost children, bereft parents, and the world
are all watching for signs and portents,
trying to make sense of a puzzle of missing pieces,
looking for a message, a messiah, for meaning.

My ten-year-old attaches a note as he wraps
his grandmother's Christmas present – an ornament,
a small angel carrying a lantern labeled "hope."
He places it in a large decorative bag and writes:
"We are a small people in a big world."

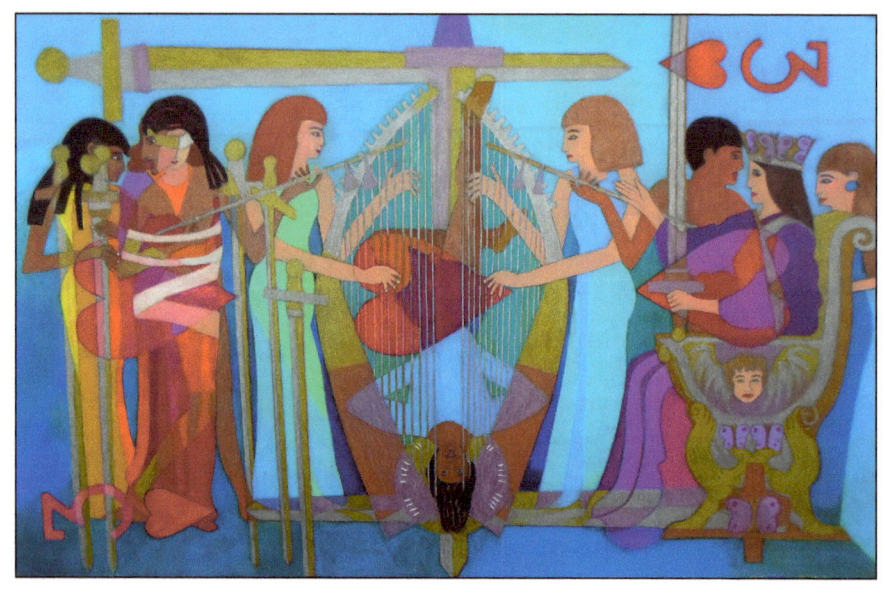

Three of Hearts Divided
26 x 40 inches, 2012

The card and poem are both about the tricks our hearts play on us, our fickle natures,
and our tendency to judge others more severely than we judge ourselves in matters of the heart.

Funhouse Heart

The door opens to pericardia darkness, the warm moist air
assaults you like August at Coney Island. The floor moves,
throwing you off your feet and into the right atrium,
where you are barrel-rolled through a spinning passage.

Unbalanced and unnerved, you drop into the right ventricle,
groping your way to the stairs that shake and shimmy,
climbing past distorted reflections, completely confused
and gasping for air, you are expelled onto the fairway.

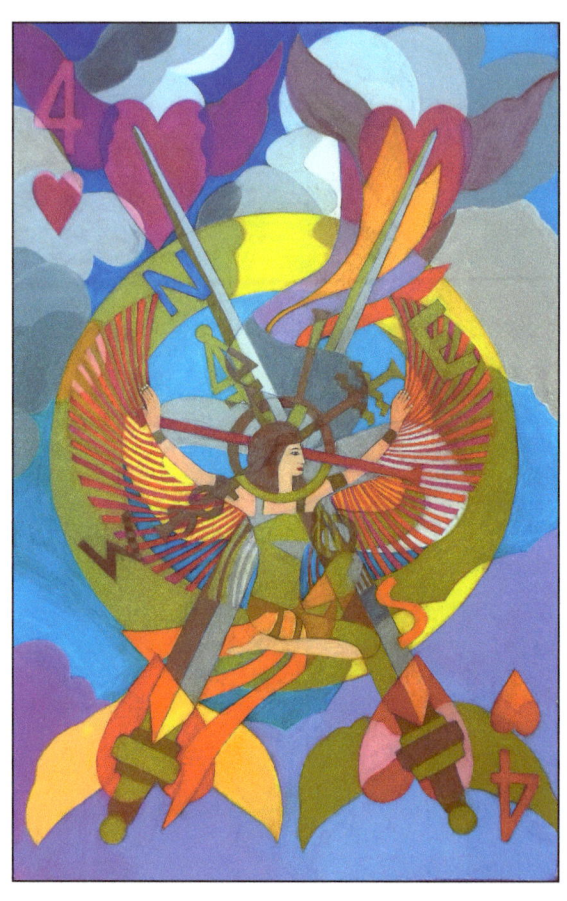

On the Four Winds Does My Heart Fly
40 x 26 inches, 2013

On the Four Winds Does My Heart Fly

The wheel turns, the sun rises
on New Year's Day, and on the four
winds does my heart fly to friends
near, far, and long departed.

First it travels north to the land
of snow and winter winds, along
the shores of the Great Lakes
of Kitchi-gummi and Michi-gami.

Then it spreads wings southeast
through Texas to the trade winds,
reefs, and hurricanes, Georgia,
Jamaica, the Florida coast and Keys.

Skirting the edge of a nor'easter, it moves
along the shore to D.C., Coney Island,
Brooklyn, and Queens, up to Old Lyme
near Newtown where my heart breaks.

Gathering itself, it circles across the Atlantic
to Paris, back to the Cape, Provincetown,
Trujo, and Wellfleet, crossing the bridge
inland to Brockton, Amherst, Springfield.

Spinning east through the Ohio Valley
across through Gary, Chicago, and
Tornado Alley, it soars up the Rockies
to Aspen, Woodland Park, and Denver.

A gust tosses my heart across Nebraska,
then reverses to Montana, then down
to Eugene, California, out to Thailand
and back again, pausing in San Diego.

At long last it turns east towards
Albuquerque on the prevailing winds.

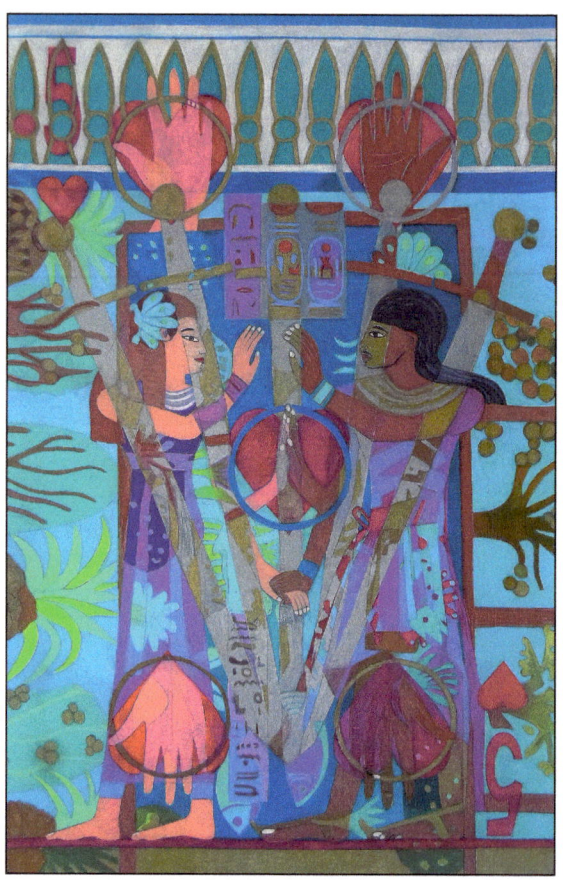

Five of Ringing Hearts
40 x 26 inches, 2013

Five Rings

Five fingers on each hand,
and no rings on any finger
for my hands are always
typing, working, covered
with pigment and ink.

I once had a ring of gold
and rubies, first on my
left hand, then on a chain
around my neck, now
nestled in the box next
to the three rings you
always wore: wedding,
signet, and mother's ring.

The fifth ring from Hawaii,
your brother gave you
to repose in a silent
rose garden where now
my father's ashes also rest.

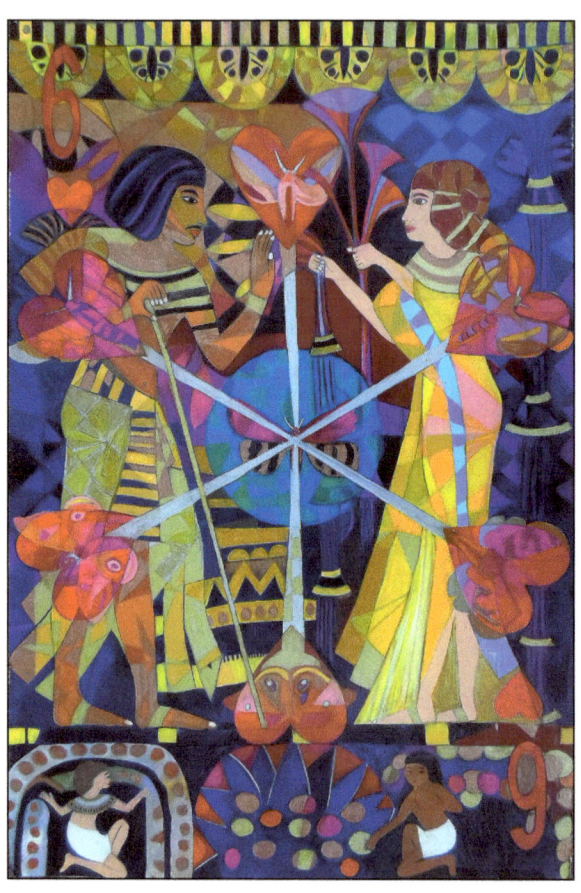

Six Phases of the Eclipse of the Heart
40 x 26 inches, 2013

Six Phases of the Eclipse of the Heart

With moths fluttering in changing dark,
the moon moving through six phases
of lunar eclipse, our clandestine shadows
meet to bid each other a final farewell
and fade from earth into the long night.

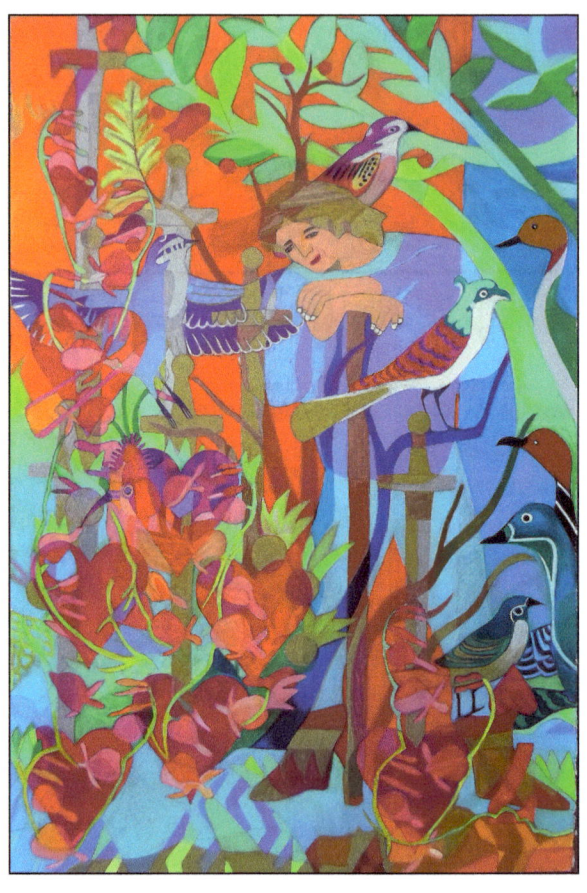

Seven of Flowering Hearts
40 x 26 inches, 2013

My father was a great gardener, who spent his life as a counselor and social worker,
so in the card he is caring for the pierced hearts, which begin to flower under his care.
The poem reflects on the mysterious processes of cyclical birth and rebirth in the garden and in life.

Secret Garden

In the fall, a new gardener
turned the soil in unfamiliar
earth, disturbing hidden roots
of dormant plants that long ago
another had planted and watered,
until in the midst of long drought,
stem, branch, and leaf disappeared,
the gardener vanished and the garden
waited in the dark ground to break
open to sunlight, wind, and rain,
until in the spring the gardener
returns, startled by flowers.

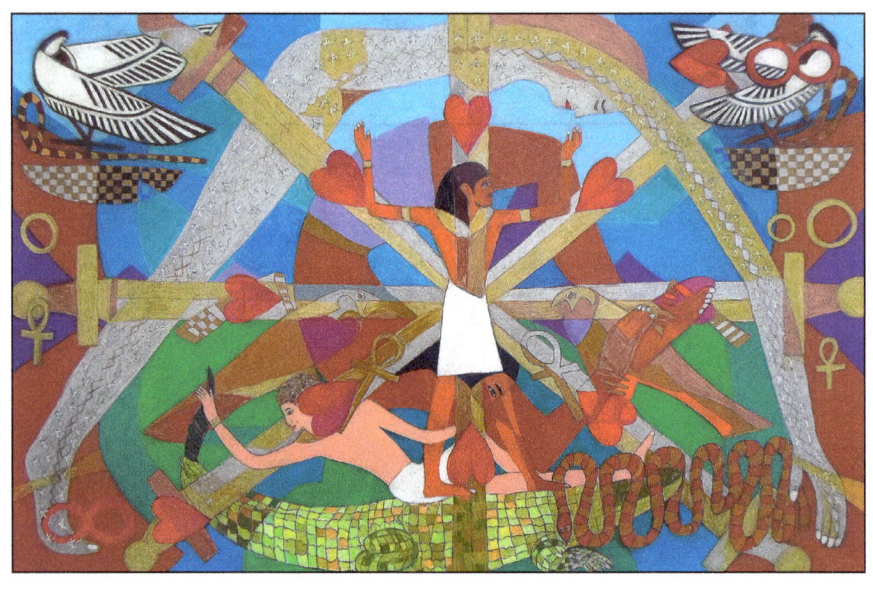

Eight of Infinite Hearts
26 x 40 inches, 2013

In the card my sons are again navigating life on the back of a crocodile, while I am shielding them from above in the guise of the Egyptian sky goddess Nut and their father protects them from below as the acrobatic figure in the background. The poem reflects on this dangerous adventure called life.

Rafting the River

You embark at the point when
you no longer know what to do,
carrying all that you love, allowing
the current to take you where it will.

You will encounter white water,
waves, rocks, hazards, sudden drops,
and severe impacts, risking grave
injury and death, but oh the ride!

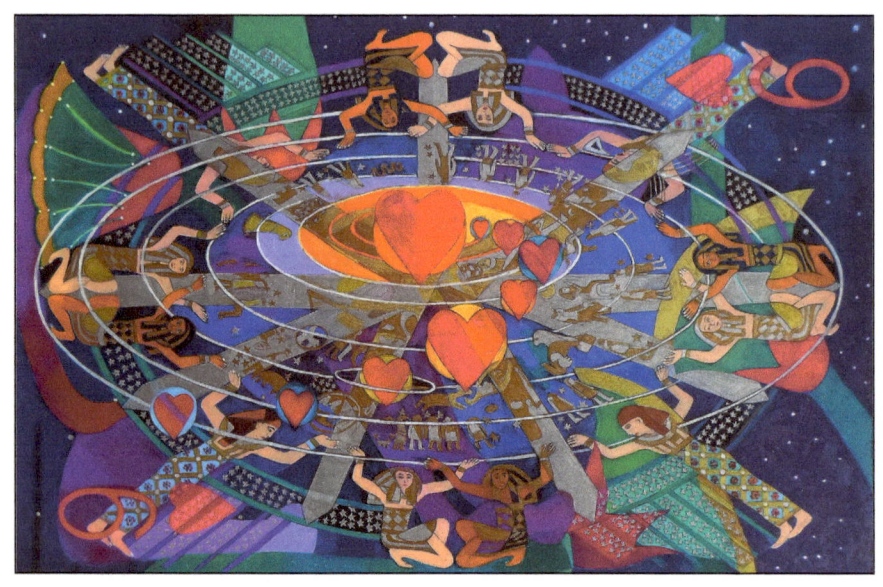

The Nine Lives of the Heart
26 x 40 inches, 2013

Inspired by an Egyptian painting of the universe, my sons and I are working hard
to keep our family's universe spinning with the "nine lives" of the heart forming the sun
and the eight planets. The poem reflects on the havoc the forces of nature play on our lives.

Solar Wind

Every day Earth greets solar wind,
streaming a million miles an hour
past our planet, shifting flights
into unforeseen trajectories,
forming aurora borealis, and
reversing the paths of comets.

Last night I listened to the desert wind,
howling seventy miles an hour past
my door, crashing the trashcans,
shaking the dry branches, twigs,
and leaves from the trees, spawning
dust devils on the mesa.

This morning I remember the wind,
as seasons rage, spawning tornadoes
spinning across the Midwestern Plains
ripping off housetops, demolishing
Main Streets of Midwest towns like
Greensburg, Parson, and Joplin.

In my dreams the wind lifts me flying
across mountains, plains, and out to sea,
my mind a hurricane of thoughts,
my body a whirlwind of emotion,
and we meet again for an instant
silently in the eye before the wind
flings us into the maelstrom.

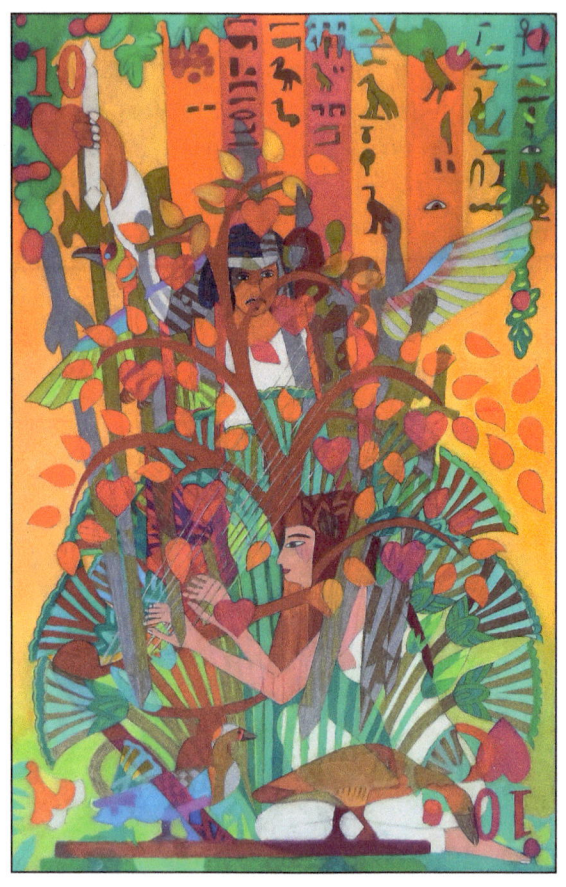

The Ten Strings of My Heart
40 x 26 inches, 2013

The card portrays the romance between myself, the harpist, and my husband, the magician.
The poem reflects on the intimate connection that survives distance, time, and even death.

String Theory

A strand drawn immeasurably thin
stretches between us; when you accidentally
brush your finger across it, disturbing my sleep
with its silent hum, I wake, calling out your name.

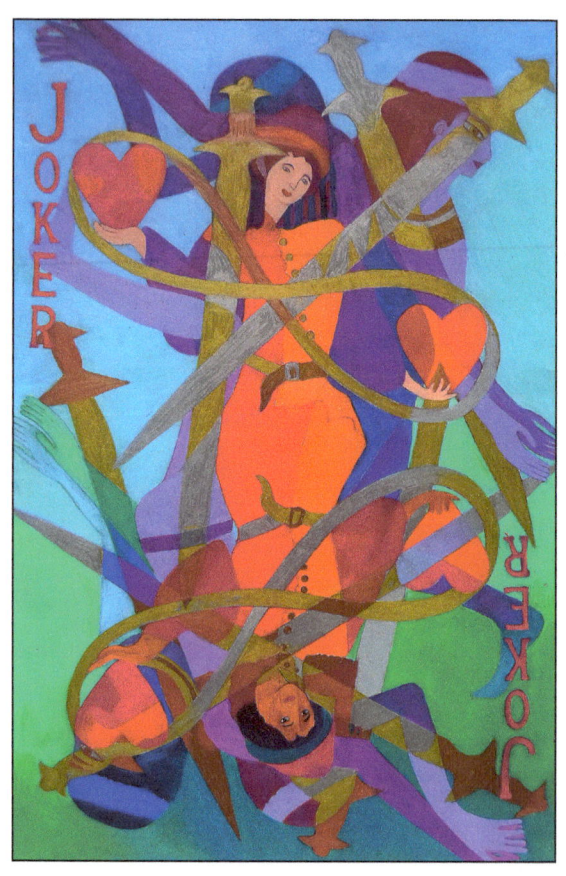

The Joke's on Our Hearts
40 x 26 inches, 2013

Jugglers

Knives spin,
sharp edges glint,
hearts in our hands,
we dance while swords
rain endlessly around us.

www.ingramcontent.com/pod-product-compliance
Lightning Source LLC
Chambersburg PA
CBHW041611180526
45159CB00002BC/807